A History of the Sweetness of the World

The *Texas Review* Southern and Southwestern Writers
Breakthrough Series introduces outstanding work of talented new poets
and fiction writers from the South and Southwest.

General Editors:
Paul Ruffin, Sam Houston State University
George Garrett, University of Virginia

A History of the Sweetness

of the World

By

Michael Lieberman

1995 Winner
The *Texas Review* Southern and Southwestern Poets
Breakthrough Series

Texas Review Press
Huntsville, Texas

FIRST EDITION, 1995

Requests for permission to reproduce material from this work should be sent to:

Permissions
Texas Review Press
English Department
Sam Houston State University
Huntsville, TX 77341

Some of these poems initially appeared, often in a slightly different form, in the following publications: *Amelia, American Literary Review, Borderlands, Hawai'i Review, A Language We Know At Once, The Midwest Quarterly, Potato Eyes, Prairie Schooner, Sulphur River Literary Review, Tampa Review, The Texas Review,* and *Webster Review.* The epigraph in "Cities" is from *Selected Poems,* by Osip Mandelshtam (Selected and translated by James Greene), Penguin Books, London, 1991.

Library of Congress Cataloging-in-Publication Data

Lieberman, Michael, 1941—
       A history of the sweetness of the world / by Michael Lieberman.—
    1st ed.
              p.   cm. — (The Texas Review southern and southwestern poets
       breakthrough series)
          ISBN 1-881515-06-0 (hardback). — ISBN 1-881515-07-9 (paper)
          I. Title. II. Series
       PS3562.I434H57   1995
       811'.54—dc20

To Susan,
Jonathan and Seth

Table of Contents

—A Slender Decency—

—The Mint and Perfumes We Carry—

—A Language We Are Afraid to Understand—

A History of the Sweetness

of the World

A Slender Decency

Los Olivos

for Ron Serrano (1941-1964)

The olive trees grow silently in patches on the shoulders
of this town with its roll of ocher and California oak.
The palms droop over the earth as if to scoop up the air
which hesitates and stammers as it rises. The tongue
of the afternoon is too parched to speak. Suddenly my wife
mentions you, and I realize they should have buried you here
in the dry land, on top of a small mesa as if it were
an altar to offer up your presence above the fields and ranches
where irrigation matters, where your knowledge
of flow and turbulence would count for something.
What has been spoken under the rose between you two
over thirty years is unclear. What is unspoken between us
is that I married the woman you should have married,
fathered the children you should have fathered.
It is I who watch the hawks dizzy themselves
as if their calculated drift upward could bring rain
to this land beyond the coastal range.
I do not believe you soar with those hawks—or anywhere—
nor do you rest. But evanescent gods may watch over you
who are now mostly the water you dreamed of.
Surely if there is grace, they would bestow it
on a giver of water. They would come forward
to bless your graphs and equations.
I see the crimson bougainvillea in aneurysmal bursts
along the railroad and think of the explosion in your skull
and how simple mechanical failure has left me
to honor you as you had honored me in your choosing.

On the Anniversary of My Father's Death

I scoop up fine sand with the plastic shovel
of a small boy, funnelling it over you
in pinions. Grasp her tail feathers, father,
rise with the heat. Surge through dark veins
to their last branchings. Forget Helbros watches.

Roll the desk top down, leave Pittsburgh,
its gritty window sills. Let your silver body
rise up so I can feel the withered muscles
of your back. Make love to the show girl
from Las Vegas you have dreamed of.

Dailiness sucked your large brightness to a dry
socket. Stretch yourself out on the flatness
of the world—let this tribute draw the terror
from you. Seventeen years too late, I am arriving
indecently with the covered dish I owe you.

How can I find you, not below a proper Jewish
headstone in the high Reform cemetery, but where
you pitch and yawl, longing to trim your body
out of turbulence, unless I release myself
from the stubble to a dry dispersing wind?

Homage in Kind

for Weldon Kees, after an observation by Kenneth Rexroth

His poems rendered darkness, love of trope
in form as subtle as bas-relief on a frieze.
A modern man at the end of his rope,

he edged us to a rim and down a slope:
with one soft tap we buckled at the knees,
seduced by darkness, love of trope,

as lines went slack then taut in swells to cope
with limbic dredgings from cerebral seas.
A modern man at the end of his rope,

he glimpsed our folly—not as misanthrope—
as prey of furies no one could appease.
Secured by darkness, love of trope,

he sealed compassion in an envelope
without address or stamp. His dis-ease,
a modern man at the end of his rope.

When chemistry undid each glint of hope,
snuffed out the miner's light of Weldon Kees,
his poems shone in darkness, love of trope;
resurrected a man at the end of his rope.

Survivor

Cadmium, leper of metals,
unable to shed the stigma of its birth.
As Primo Levi wrote *The Periodic Table,*
he willfully avoided this survivor—
only to have the mind's alchemy
transmute uranium, unearth the past,
convey it to the surface of a story.
For forty years he battled the slither
of fascism each night, the eye
of that furnace consuming him.
By day he managed tales of grace
and wit to placate the beast, books,
an earnest column for *La Stampa.*
But in his poems the metallic taste
stains through—life *longer than anyone
ever lived*, he wished Adolph Eichmann.
The entwining compels—one event
wrapped around another. Cadmus
squeezed, gasping for breath, stripped
of ascent. And Levi, finally without luster,
hammered into a vessel of assent.

The Future

Soon the school boy who cannot remember
his tables will be the old Jew struggling
to recall all the commandments, swaying
at prayers in a wooden *shul* in Poland.

*The future is a contract to cut Count Novatny's
forests*, he thinks. He is fingering
his prayer book, mumbling the past, his hands
already gripping the ax. If he imagines
the Almighty, the cedars brought to Jerusalem
to build the Temple, he does not let on.

He prays, bending at the waist
and straightening with the motion of a bird
pecking. If there is gleaning to be done,
he does not do it. Great grandfather says,
for ten zlotys I will tell you the future—

*how the branches will be trimmed, the bark
stripped and the boards loaded onto wagons.
Never mind,* I say, *I am the future,
tell me about the past.*

Lynchburg

Not Jack Daniels' town in Tennessee.
Beryl Eichelbaum's city in Virginia.
He came steerage, carried a pack
through the Blue Ridge and peddled dry goods.
He settled among Jerry Falwell's ancestors,
lived between the furrows God raked
north to south in some mysterious plan
for America, traded horses, bought and sold
scrap metal in the Bible Belt.
Our family says he smuggled livestock
on the Polish-Russian border, that he came
alone in the eighteen-eighties and sent
for his wife Rebecca, my great grandmother,
in eighteen-ninety-four. They lived there,
raised children in a white frame house
surrounded by lilacs and Baptists,
in the shadow of Manassas, Shiloh.

In the tiny Jewish Cemetery their headstones
stand today—abandoned by family
who moved to Richmond, Norfolk,
by the dissolving rain of history. Dead
sixty years among the plantain and dandelions.
The weeds choke off their voices,
obscure our view of the common grace
of their survival. I travel there each spring
when the redbud clings close, when I can
imagine pushing through the undergrowth
of dogwood to arrive at their ordinary

lives. No one remains for *Kaddish.*
I pray a holy spirit to pass through, to stop,
to make a small sign to remember them.

Hobart Street

My mother is filled with desires she cannot speak:
llamas, creatures from the steppes and savannahs.

At seventy-three she does not tell me what she waits for.
She sits alone, without birds or flowers, looking out

at the melting snow, gray with the gnarl of Pittsburgh.
When the mist settles, it is like ash, the flecks

drifting down on her apartment. My mother waits
at the window for a knight riding a llama.

Small birds cannot peck at the feeder she has not
set out on the ledge of brick and brindled mortar.

She imagines she rolls her desires in a blanket,
hoists this bedroll behind the knight's saddle,

rides with him to the small house on Hobart Street.
He waits by the curb where the ice has cleared.

She is a young girl going to the closet, finding
her sister has taken the white dress with the ruffles,

the hairbrush with the bone handle. She brushes
her hair in the empty house with her mother's brush.

The knight waits while my mother searches for
her white sandals, my father, her parents, her children.

She is at the window leaning on the cracked sill,
looking at her bedroll, precious and soiled, behind the saddle.

He offers nothing. My mother turns away,
trying to remember what she desires.

My Father

let the mucus plug his throat,
the monitor go haywire then flat,
not out of yearning for expansive otherness,
but from conviction, as a gift.

No infusion of adrenaline
could clear this fuzz of logic from his mind.
He misplaced duty as a salesman
would lay down an order book—all the while

sure he could remember every item.
He was convinced he would profit little
buying up odd lots from drab store fronts,
selling one-onlies in the wholesale district.

His departure—how delicate this word feels
on the tongue—would release my sister
from a man she married in obedient defiance,
release my brother, me.

My father would wander free, untethered—
an orbiter flung off on a tangent of his choosing.
He would not be a burden—a bag of ready mix
soaked in the driveway and hardening.

His intern, Harry, I still remember his earnest face,
said my father was strong, remarkable.
What codicil, I ask, convinced the blood
in his coronaries to sludge and clot?

He quit, went over to an unknowable place
after sitting in our living room one winter,
listening over and over to songs from the Civil War,
sobbing, unable or unwilling to explain.

Ascent

A point of departure is a Mozart andante
from a concerto numbered in the high teens or twenties,
valleys of rhododendron and choke cherry,
not cobble stones on icy hills, not Pittsburgh,
horses pulling Braddock's wagons,
prayers for safe descent, curses, movement
of corn and whisky to the rivers. Traction.
Iron in the valleys, on wheel rims.
Beauty as clarity, as cortege,
ascent of shallow grades.
Not his masses, not *Exultate Jubilate*, but andantes.
Whole notes as Texas leaguers,
half notes as cracked buckeyes,
resolution as weathered gravestones.
These are the marks he made
as Presbyterians etched Western Pennsylvania,
before Bessemer furnaces filled every crack with soot.
His was ascent as Dante imagined,
without grime, without words or destination,
only turbulence in the clear air.

Hearing Auden Read

These days without the Soviets and Yugoslavia,
with Northern Ireland, there is so much talk about Europe.
It is good to remember what he mentioned with a prisoner's

conviction: *poetry makes nothing happen* . . . In this he
was right, nothing is the praise of one apparition
for another. Was it winter or fall or spring, 1960 or 1961,

that he read in New Haven? He appeared,
large and solemn as granite, exposed against the varnished
oak walls, an Englishman from Mt. Rushmore.

Sensing the dull surfaces of undergraduates,
he bounced his lines off us. Through open windows
horns dopplered down Whitney Avenue, but he picked out

his sounds unaltered returning to him. He stood with a long face,
a dignified stork, giving no idea of his migratory patterns.
He had lit down, and, looking out, tried to say a few things plainly.

That night he appeared like an eclipse we don't quite remember—
an experience when subtraction adds—and left us
with a negative afterimage. What we recorded

was the size of his task, but mostly we wondered
how we would earn a living. He knew working by deletion
is slow, that it takes decades to make nothing happen.

Why Should I Clone the Genes of Simon Srebnik?

What would I understand if I knew
the sequence of his DNA, could place
him in perspective with Cro-Magnon,
patriarchs, his ancestors, my ancestors?
If I knew his story in detail?
Nine hours of "Shoah" is a man singing, a Jew,
in soft focus in a small boat on a small river
in the morning. He is drifting by mounds
of coarse hair and shoes in my living room.
A Jew in a boat. A Jew in a boat
singing in Polish is beyond oscilloscopes.
I am humming a song I cannot hear,
a melody I do not know, accompanying
a man remembering a youth he does not remember.
He is impounded on a reel of tape,
trying to moor a past in the present.
With a warble older than the song, he frames
a sweetness measured only in angstroms.

My Son's Name

My semen conjured in your mother's womb.
No moon, no street lights, nothing moved.
Silence sat on the ledge, listened
to you thrash in the mucus.

At first I couldn't tell your crowning
from her sex: red fire then a singe of hair,
you squinted defiance as they cut you free,
faced down tubes and nurses,
clenched your name against your chest,
whispered it to me in the heavy snow that followed.

Seth—I think of the blow of the sea
at Mustang Island. Dunes festooned with flowers,
morning glories closing over sounds,
the rap and crash of waves, the hammer
of Cain on Abel, the foam receding
on its sandpiper feet.

Sealed in a Mason jar it sat,
no crust of sugar, no ooze of juice,
nothing was let out. No one could crack
the lid that hid its meaning in plain view,
chaperoned its cling- or freestone nature.

I went out this morning early, began
pulling chickweed from the cracks,
piling it in mounds of trash,
divined these entrails, found

a history of your naming:
a root hair lanced ancestral granite,
a thread too fine to draw out anything,
the purchase one or two cells thick.

I watched silence lift your name,
drop its essence
as a gull would break a shell,
and veer in the *kee kee kee* of the wind.

Dislocations

Your name shall no longer be Jacob,
but Israel, for you have striven with beings
divine and human, and have prevailed.
                                    —Genesis, 32

I think of this morning as the morning after,
as if I've just made love all night to God
and have prevailed. Women can permeate
the woody center of things like a preserving resin,
but men must prevail; so I speak to shed my skin,
to examine articulations, how the body of our belief is joined.

Last night while Jacob wrestled, I made love
to goddesses who coalesced around a single name.
Aphrodite, they called themselves, born of the sea foam.
To possess her, I married the wind.

Wrenched at the hip, I threw away my crutch,
leaned on the transubstantial, listed from one position
to another, used all the arms of Shiva
to embrace every goddess and all her daughters.
I hammered on the breast plate of Athena,
forced the release of Mentor.

My paramours provided gentile names.
They called me *Walking on water, Playing with fire,*
Dervish of the wind. They shouted *Leave the earth, dreary*
with commercial strip and soy beans.

You might humor me with the promissory kiss
of a teething child and ask what provisions

I have made in the aftermath of so much union:
none for my soul, none for a sure and certain hope
of resurrection, none for a decent burial.

What to carry forward? The rectitude of uncertainty,
the monotheism of doubt that takes many forms:
avatars of reason, a geodesic dome—caging us off
from real animals on the ridges of the moon—
love of walking with fire as others walk with God,
the conviction that struggle is praise, that there is
a slender decency in ambiguous acts of praise.

Earth Tones

Israel, 1992

The small bones of the hand
cannot wait for rain,
for weather to erode the flint shale,
for stones, scattered on dry ridges,
to collect themselves as cairns.
They tine and furrow plateaus
for wheat, set out melon plants
like stars before the sun is high.

In some future time
archaeologists will say,
They were gatherers of stones
after they were dispersed
and gathered. This was the way
they remembered: with metered water,
grafted stock, and premixed fertilizer.

Before the Turks, before the Crusades,
Mohammed ascended from the Temple ruins,
the trees already old on the Mount of Olives.
And before, the wheat of the Hebrews,
and before wheat was the millet of the Canaanites.
And before millet, hoes and bones.

Jericho

Dizzy Gillespie and Wynton Marsalis never wailed here.
The naked trumpet of *Aida* never burst forth
in fire here, but once there was victorious music—
Joshua, hawk-faced and muscular, forced its walls
into resonant compliance. From Jerusalem the path
runs by young boys on donkeys, rubble,
the splendid blue of an Armenian monastery
to the gravel bottom of Wadi Kelt. In January, Jericho
is rich in the arid landscape—a jewel, as a burred seed
is a treasure clinging to khaki trousers.
Only the hang-dog green of last year's palms
and painted shutters warm the achromatic chill.
In the winter light Arab men are clasping cups of coffee
to outdoor tables, pushing them deliberately like chessmen
across a landscape. The game is slow. Temperatures
fall in the dusk. Mostly there are no people, only walls
concealing imagined lives waiting for grapes and wisteria
to call forth fragrance and the fields beyond the town.
Nothing can be gleaned from the fields or streets—
only from newspapers written by others from their own gleanings
of fields and streets. Nothing except that lushness is relative—
like stripes of oak in the Central Valley of California—
that history and water are what matter, that self-determination
is what we crave and can never have. A wind tumbles
over the lip of the plateau. Gabriel clears saliva
from his trumpet and offers a song to approaching night.

I Was Not There

It is true, I am the one you seek,
but there is some mistake,
I am not Ivan, I was not there,
I was in Berlin, I was Eichmann's driver;
I spent the war, my engine idling,
waiting to take him to a farm.
Before I'd been a groom for Chmielnicki;
I walked his horse and sponged him down.

After that I can't remember,
but I know I was not there,
I was assigned to Yugoslavia and Greece—
only as an aide—I can prove it.
I was attached to the SS
and served an information officer,
an Austrian who liked to ride.
I personally gelded a colt for him.
Here is my proof: All these years
I've saved them in this jar.

After the war I escaped to Palestine.
Yes, I am Ukrainian by birth,
but there the similarity ends.
Most of what I did is in your archives—
you can read them—just minor roles,
I helped Begin blow the King David,
and other odds and ends.
Last year I slipped from my cell
and joined the boys in Tunis;

my role with al Wazir was minor,
but in open court I hold my tongue;
anyway you know it from your records.

So now let's have some sport.
Suppose we steal the King's
Arabians and blind them.
I have fifty good ideas how.

Cities

But one rib of mine is a burning spike
Which isn't guarded by these watching phantoms,
Nor by this sentry asleep under the storm.
                    —Osip Mandelshtam

It is summer—when else in Houston
is it possible to remember you, Osip?
The mockingbird has gone from the wire
taking his trills, leaving the oaks—
a measly landscape.
Among the sparrows and the jackdaws there is room.

Your city was always a *might*,
a foster mother of soapstone, the *if*
of a life at the edge, the *maybe* of women.
A wasp laid her eggs in your pupa.
A gnawing harvested despair.
When the ice thawed,
the Neva's waters flowed from you.
Jew, poet, your exile began at your birth.

Like fireflies, you and Akhmatova
traced auroras in the night,
spiraled in steeples of delight—
she suckled you,
founder of your own great city.
Still, in the end, it was your wife
who boarded the faded railway car
and followed you into the alien steppes.

              *   *   *

When Voronezh squeezed the chemicals from your brain,
you tapped your message out on the barrel head of night,
created in form a land with fine contours,
extruded a bleakness we only thought we could imagine,
that had nothing to do with landscape. Alighieri gone
from Florence, Ovid from Rome, Catullus gone
to Asia Minor, gone, oozing from the contusions of your heart
in this city where we live.

        *   *   *

How extraordinary that the two of you—he in his great fur coat
    and miter
and you dressed in what friends provided—struggled for the soul
    of Russia.
If you were alive today, you would know that neither of you won:
the sorghum mill of enmity grinds silage from Russians who are
    not Russian.
He has been dead forty years and you for almost sixty—all parties
are still in place, their voices shrill in the dust. Your sentence is
    still in force.

        *   *   *

They splashed water on your face—
sons who did not know you—
took a blunt knife to you,
dismembered you on a cloudy night,
rubbed the stumps of your poems
in the black earth of the steppes.
Three women gleaned them
from the fields, carried them

like embryos inside themselves,
resurrected you—alien and Russian Jew,
a Russian prince on other continents.

        *   *   *

Osip, what is left besides pitted surfaces and fissures
in the speckled sun, a weathering so severe it has stunted
the trees and pocked the face of your beloved city?

We both know that no abrasive can grind this surface clean,
the best we can hope for is a rough approximation,
that we can mill the tolerance our calipers demand.

Sometimes the carborundum of the living
works better than a grinding stone. It may provide
a finish, lusterless and rough, but a finish still.

Different justices today compete—all capricious or incomplete;
let our lichen vision grow, sessile on the fascist sore,
a flowerless pigment on a stone and ideologically impure.

The Mint and Perfumes We Carry

Dark Against the Snow

Coinage comes hard, the currency of thought,
the imprinting of blank discs,
transformations to tokens, specie.

Think of Silhouette overseeing the franc,
fleeing the Bourse, leaving only his shadow
for the doves on telephone lines to cast

on the dirty snow, giving themselves over
to tenderness, their outlines eclipsing
the sun, forcing the light within

to concentrate itself and pour out.
Where will the bartering end, the exchange
of one realm for the next?

The Condition of Being

If only we were acellular, not prodded by heat,
not in need of water and ions, if we were unresponsive
to light, perhaps if we were molecules—large ones,
say proteins, and only rotated and folded in response
to rules, if we did not reproduce, if joy did not shower
blindly at the lifting of large birds or obligation
force us under sagging bridges with our shoulders;
if we were only electrons seeking escape, but caught
by nuclear forces, degraded by collisions,
subject only to chance, not likely to be on corners
during drive-by shootings or a constituent of coke
or angel dust . . . then we could hope for change, take
a positive position in spite of charge, lobby for inclusion
in a vaccine, save a life and allow it to remain
in the universe of strange forces to undergo the pressures
of being, emerge on the streets with a grade school education,
with only raw need, without skill, to take chances
in a gang or work for minimum wage in a world of movies
and colored television, then we would be free to let
the random govern, to be sovereigns of our impoverished selves.

Arpeggios

We wish for arpeggios—
disassembly of the unruly into intelligible parts—
siphon, gut, osseous shell.
Not to be pried open and shucked
by muscular fingers with short knives,
molested with a grain of sand.
But to be untangled as one would stems of coreopsis.

If there can be no unity,
let there be a harmony of parts,
plucked one by one, with resonance.
If not a harmony of parts,
burial after autopsy
with clear data on our murders.

If we cannot be buried with horns and trumpets
as Wagner and Bruckner, as Mahler especially
would have wished—the sonorous tow
of middle Europeans—then let us exult in splinters,
accept a fracture that will not heal,
a stump leaving only concertos for one hand,

embrace resolution as a disparate stream of parts
arriving by timetables.
Peonies before chrysanthemums.
Buses choked on the wrong highway and late.
Let each sound tumble into rays, pistils, stamens, colors—
a fragrance porous to the traffic of the world.

Eleven Views from the Bayou at Chimney Rock

1

What happened before words,
when the heart squeezed
meaning from our blood,
when oleander bloomed—first red
then white, spread
like lilies on the bayou?

2

Given the clouds
obscuring the stars,
our only choice
is oleander—
serrations,
white and delicate,
encircling.

3

Oleander, astride the bayou,
crazed from within,
self-feeder,
head tossed back in the wind.

How to skirt her ragged dance,
the greed that drives the mouth
to strip free the bark
and lick the alkaloids of loss.

4

Oleander is not
the extravagant answer.

The peonies
flow, ruffled
like a young boy's foreskin.

5

The bayou cleaves
live oak from live oak
cottonwood from cottonwood
loquat from loquat—
two hemispheres
of like mind.

6

Yes, the whippet, we wait
for the lesser arc,
her midriff baled,
snout drawn out from molten glass,

for her acceleration, accurate,
into herself
that says *wait*—which is
what we do at Chimney Rock.

7

Clouds, dark as greyhounds,
lean into their gait,
overfly, swirl back.
Skewers of salvia nose the air.
Stragglers, ribs heaving,
muzzle-loaded, are plenteous
on the eaves and hard pan.

8

Rubble barge, I tow you
up the bayou, aloft,
a braid of rope over my shoulder,
mad with the buzz
of concrete embankments,
the connivance of murky water,
the factious grass.

9

Flower of the dark eye,
reciprocal of stars,

earthbound, ovarian,
fly up.

Annihilate your mirror self.
Canes of blackberry flow
where you watched the bayou.

10

Lantana, relentless
among the thorns,
each round lingers
like a tracer.
Fire a salvo
across my bow.
Board me.

11

See the oleander huddle in the rain,
unctuous, close.
What can you possibly offer blossoms
turned dower, spillways
eyeing our rush to the sea?
Star burst in my eclipse,
what pain if I should touch
even the camisole of your small breasts.

Vision

By the curb where I turn left to work
something has stripped a cedar of its needles,
exposed the saprophytes—spinous urchins
suspended like flecks in the turquoise of morning.

If a griffin should perch in that cedar,
I would ignore it.
If I had the eye of a hawk,
I would see with it.

My heart would empty with each systole.
Your body would be a memory-trace.
Only my axons would quiver.
I would get down on my hands and knees
and thank God for color vision.

Loss

The arroyo was filled with fine
dry sand. It was autumn.

I invited the gods to make love to me
under the bridge. Their thick beards

were splendid in the filtered light.
They filled me with hope, left me

by the fire with a pencil stub and tablet
to write a history of the sweetness

of the world, the sweetness of the world
reduced to a pile of yellow sheets.

The light will curl their corners to a past.
I am leaving with what I brought—

a sack of desperate silence—and my notes.
If the gods with their heft return,

wait for the cottonwoods to yellow,
offer them only a trinket or the sand.

Wedge this in a mullion of your window;
it is a picture of me when I was young.

Regret

One day you will slip into an airport,
stride past the phones, jingling your change,
and toss your hanging case into a cab.
You will feel only the slightest twinge
as you realize that I live in that city—
in good health, but old and somewhat frail—
that you will see me alive
perhaps a dozen times more,
and then only in orchestrated visits.
You will give a small shudder of regret
and move on. On that day you
will have learned what I have taught you.

At Autopsy

The back and buttocks are the color
of Santa Rosa plums, the detail is there—
even the fine speckling, as if the surface
were splashed intentionally,
as a wood spirit might bruise a foxglove.

The arms and legs stiffen with a standard text,
a consorting of calcium and ATP—
this to be ignored like junk mail.
A vaulted room of white tile and grout,
an apron impervious to fluid.

My business is weighing organs,
dismembering tissues that sort themselves out
only in their dying. It is not as hard
as you might imagine to tell the past
from the past. To see the future

I excise the eye of the snake,
pour the glow of its retina over my own,
stroke its pleated belly tailwise,
and pray for resolution, for the narrow
spectrum of light assigned to us all.

Deluxe Post Mortem

We are a full service laboratory—
chemistry, hematology, microbiology.

We inspect tattoos and dental work,
check for open sores and bruises.

We check for parasites, provide
your loved ones with complete details

of our examination from the first incision
to the weighing and slicing of organs.

With our report we send computer scans
of microscopic slides and pictures

of the convolutions of your brain.
We examine seven different regions

from the brain; upon request these sections
can be stained with gold or silver.

We can leave the eyes in place
or substitute pure crystal globes.

We save bits of you in formalin
and soon will offer cryopreservation.

Your body will be closed with fine silk sutures.
We provide a shroud of Egyptian cotton.

Unfailingly we gather a *minyan*
to chant the Jewish prayer for the dead.

Without Allusion

I'd like to report a honeysuckle sighting,
near a Texaco in Chapel Hill,
just off the red clay shoulder of Elliott Road,
a vine of yellow and white flowers
clustered over blackberry and small oaks,
a quarter mile from a vacant lot
where catalpa and magnolia are blooming.
I walked over from the macadam and smelled.
Honeysuckle, I say,
I'm reporting honeysuckle,
I'm sure,
it reminds me of nothing else.

Offering

When Icarus fell into the flat forever of Texas, his body jack-knifed over the Reardons' fence. The drone of the afternoon tried not to notice. His life rushed out. Three Tejanos gathered his wings for angels at the church. Roberto smoothed them into plastic bags, imagined tacking them in place to mask the cracking plaster, a little extra help for Christ at Easter. Pedro blotted up the sweat with a polka dot bandanna; he would soak it in the baptismal font. *When Father Alfonso baptizes my daughter tomorrow*, he thought, *she will receive this body. Azules*, murmured Rolando, *blue. His eyes are blue, this man-bird.* He thought of buzzards, the yellow-eyed owls. *Only anglos have blue eyes. Jesus should have had blue eyes. What use*, he wondered. *Where to store them—the church, the barn, the Reardons' house, his own house. Azules*, he had seen these eyes glazed on Indian pots, strange animals, half human. Before he could remove his knife, Becky Reardon knelt down, kissed the lids and repeated, *Azules. Sus ojos son azules.* They wrapped the body in a quilt and then a horse blanket, buried it before Hank returned, and marked the grave with a large stone. Father Alfonso did not read. *Angels sing their own requiems*, he said. Beyond the barn the cotton boiled white in the bottom of abundant updrafts and pushed past the river and the other bank to the far edge of the land where the earth itself is blue, where nothing is embodied.

Prediction

The world might end in crispness
like a smack on the bottom at birth.
A division of skin or fascia at autopsy.
The closing of doors, the departure
of planes. Endings without confetti.
An unpeddled note on a harpsichord.

I think the world will end in Houston.
Mold, an extrusion of hyphae on formica.
Accretion of residues and gels. As a mollusk.
Even aluminum will rust. Small animals
will decompose, ferns will grow, pterodactyls
will fly, thick as the day the world began.

A Geography of Endings

World without end they pray
    in Chicago, in Massachusetts,

trying to stave off the frost
    that gaffs chrysanthemums

and hangs the oaks
    in hoop skirts of copper.

Near Silverthorn under the aspen
    tendrils of vetch encircle nothing,

bumblebees too heavy to lift themselves
    cling like supernumerary blossoms.

Somewhere fungus brings darkness
    to the zinnias,

blackens everything but the flowers,
    each a shining glans.

In preparation I have tattooed
    the Mahabharata on my chest,

opened a door
    for the empty radiance of a cloud.

The Origin of Faith

A fine layer of grit and sand—
what is shed from the being of the world—
has collected under the hoop rug
in the rented beach house in Santa Barbara.
I lie on the oak floor waiting for them
to enter from the heavy vines and sweep
it into piles. I see fuchsia lips and white tongues
in the bougainvillea and summon the rest,
as Augustine filled in the details of the Holy Spirit
and Buddha imagined the lack of details.
I am certain only that each will use
a whisk broom and the larger one, the one
who will have wings the color of the fog
at dawn, will hold the dust pan.
They will fill small bags with it,
pause in the eucalyptus grove, devise
a plan, seek out the houses
of the partisans, and deposit it
between the sheets of restless believers.

A Language We Are Afraid To Understand

Readying

may be a matter of basalt,
tongues in the cattails of Rosetta,
the smelting of Cornish ore,
visors, javelins, manacles;

or paste wax applied to the hood,
the leaving of foam rings on glasses,
the glazing of cakes and windows,
the sanding of wood and varnish;

or preparations that are not ours—
clouds forced by winds into shapes
we wish or do not wish, the schedule
of trains, the closing of roads, rain;

and acts, the planting of bulbs,
some help from the dredge of roots,
phloem, the cooperation of light,
the cutting of a single narcissus,

the scent tumbling from the vase,
its vapor, heavy, distracting,
green limb emerging, six-petaled ray,
yellow nub of Venus rising.

Extraction

Red is burned into the night,
alone, unreachable—

sequestered in a pit of stars,
a ravenous glow of beginnings,

amputated from a lash of comet
unable to blaze to an end.

It is locked in a rose
beneath its sheen. Cinnabar

of mercury, what solvent can send
it bleeding into the streets?

Uncuring tincture of need,
last pigment from the first,

it leaves behind heavy bodies, luminous,
and the skeletons of flowers.

The stallion spills from the sky
in centipede brilliance.

Ring the bell, hoist
the pigment of this beast,

speak a language
we are afraid to understand.

Suspended Dawn

Again.
Black rim—oblongate—on jaguar skin.
Silence fenced out—and in.
Blackness is a calligraphy—punctate in its center.

The cricket winches night toward day, then stops.
Silence on silence is a canvas of black on black
stretched on a tympanic membrane—
the explanation unspoken,
waiting for patterns embroidered in light.

What we hear with the eyes closed
is not what we hear with them open—
not even in the blackness
when the drunks have ceased
and sleep has muffled the cars.

We wait—sure of the promise of light,
suspended in this eclipse,
the ellipse seared on the jaguar's skin—
for a view through the hummingbird's wing,
in the blur of the wing's white noise.

The Rim of Morning

It is also a fact
    that if the lizard

comes down
    from his scaffold

and the moon begins
    to rub itself out,

dawn will rise
    from a comma of light.

Morning in Santa Fe

It arrives like Gabriel—
in a minaret of backlit cloud
over a sway of mountain—

a hoop dancer,
a homily chanted in our cisterns,
a fleck that baffles our neurons.

Everything comes to this:
wishing the wind
would catch us up

in the swirl we call morning,
peel back the sleeve of night,
reveal you, Master, reveal you.

Morning in San Miguel

Some moons are too luminous to praise,
and so, up early, I boil water for my wife's tea.

The gong of the church is stiff with night
as it strikes six, sure and certain—then pinging

from another far below—of an average day
in irrigated fields. The sun floods the land

with radiance—too pale for farmers cinching
burros, or brailleless beggars on the stoops.

El Barco

Bark has slipped from our language
leaving us behind.

Jiménez reminds us
of great seas and small rivers, of lakes
flooded with silver, the moon
searching for us,

laying down
a path we do not choose,
the moon with its sea legs wobbling
over the water.

I sit in the bow
paddling in nineteen fifty-seven,
never expecting to arrive

or return.

La Mora

It is not the mix that jars—the Bauhaus ceiling,
the Corinthian columns, the scratchy Vivaldi.
Beneath white table cloths men are touching the knees
of women, and, Alma Mahler Gropius, I am touching yours.
Beneath the sign of the blackberry, I am touching yours.
Beneath this fruited rose of small flower, the rasp
of young thorns and deep wounding, I am touching yours.

Werfel might have brought you here. Did he, Alma?
He might have courted you right over there, you,
drinking Frascati, and he, holding a book of his poems,
paraphrasing them in English, running his fingers
down your backbone, following the line of your body,
and pausing at the cross formed by your spine and bra—
as if this were a holy place, a sign that desire itself
is sacred. Was it love, Alma, or your muse he saw?

Perhaps you glowed inside as Siena might in the fading
light. Or felt only the distant pull of the Apennines
at night. From under the gnarled pines I view this sight
and feel the fire of grappa gone down too quickly. I want
to take you to the steps of the Duomo in Firenze, buy
you a leather vest from the old women in the stalls
and carve *La Mora* and my initials across the back,
Alma Schindler Mahler Gropius Werfel.

Visiting Mycenae

There is a treachery in purity
that repels, a piling of one deed
on the next like the drywall of this city.
By October the citadel has the look
of a woman out in the sun too long.
We might wish our path strewn
with poppies from a diadem
a goddess wore at her first love-making.
But Mycenae is Diana's child.
We are left to the rounded stones
in the harsh light before the winter rains.
How tiny the fortress feels when weighed
against King Agamemnon. Diana has rubbed
the dust into Clytemnestra's pores.
Snaggles of weeds and woody plants
are her revenge. For Orestes and Electra
the landscape is a frolic: an outing,
as if they had beached their punt
and climbed the hill with a picnic lunch.
As we watch them looking for shade,
we want to say, *Don't do it, Orestes,*
take off your boater, pile another stone
on the rampart and unwrap the Stilton.

Who's to Say

When desire elbows the crowd
and strides right in, in limbic boots,
or slips up to the counter
and peers mildly over the salt,
who's to say that its sweet bud
is less fully formed than love?

When love seizes a heart
that was a dry moving part
and quickens so hummingbirds sing,
is this hippocampal sting more than need
holed up akimbo in the Hyatt?

When room service brings the towels,
who tips the señorita now upon reflection
in the shattered light of what
might be mere delight or deep affection?

If we bundle the flowers of lust
in yesterday's want ads, set them out
by the curb with the trash,
who's to say that some hunk of a deity
may not rummage through to find
a bouquet for the goddess of his dreams.

Lady Astronaut

Now she is stopped at a traffic light on NASA Road 1 watching two women push shopping carts to their cars, not thinking about trajectories or how cerulean the earth seems from the sky, about the leaking drip pan of her air conditioner, soccer shoes for her boys, Halloween costumes.

On impulse she ducks into Randalls, buys coffee cake for her office, her mind on the feature section of the *Houston Post*, an article on menopause and next to it her story—her childhood in Cedar Rapids, her degree in engineering, the navy, two children, a divorce, a remarriage.

She hands the check-out girl a twenty, puts the change in the Italian billfold Mark has given her, remembers the feud, the day her second husband yanked him down by his printed tie, the metal clipboard the officer wrote on. She recalls the back seats of Chevys by the Cedar River, college dorm rooms.

She thinks of the sun edging through copper beeches at dawn, calla lilies in her mother's parlor. She had been drawn to the English professor—her second husband had bad breath and poor timing. Mark had actually been to Venice.

Chicago, Reading Brodsky's Praise of Donne

In April leafless branches divide the sky,
partition day among unpoetic duchies,
the tiny states unable to sustain themselves,
all borders, countries without orchards or beech

and maple forests. Polygons of light
too small for even the English Sparrow's glideless
sorties. Trees distort like window gratings
scoring gray to yield mosaic flecks,

small puddles in monotone. *A dark, cold day*
summons from some unreasonable place
the first daffodils—crimp-necked
and bulbous, volcanic in their crypts.

Lucky

Every heart conceals a few small secrets
or, if full of amplitude and plenty, large ones.

I begin with a green bough, forsythia—
supple and yellow with flower.

I end there—not because I am impoverished,
but because I have it all.

I Am Assigned as Vapor

You are unbridled.
Out of your stallion breath I rise.
Steaming breath, lush
with the blood's outpouring.
I rise with your milky updrafts,
hoping for something
before the wind disperses me.

Tiresias claimed women enjoy love
nine times more than men.
Sleek, snorting, giver of life,
I will settle for this lesser portion,
gladly will I take it.

I am assigned to the air as vapor,
semen-bright droplets in the wind.
I will take it for this last moment
when my atoms caress one another,
the final instant before they
cleave to the pike of the wind.

Questions about Angels

We are compelled to ask about angels,
why they live where they do—in clusters
of neurons that direct us, in a commerce
that is not a communion, but a cascading,

a frolic—young women in a stream.
Today we are no longer given streams—
the ones we loved to imagine we could come upon
are choked by wastes and solvents.

We are left to our inward angels—and they
to us—a frenzy of receptors and transmitters,
the arborizing embrace of dendrites.
Were we ever given streams?

Who actually witnessed Diana bathing
and was pierced by rage? How manipulating
they are, how liberating, these angels of color vision,
of pleasure, who remind us that grief

is played out in the underbrush of neuroglia,
below the escarpments of our regrets.
They dance under a hemisphere of bone,
gossamer membranes covering them,

not like a veil of mourning, but as a diffuser
of the harsh light of our world.
We cannot embrace these angels as ourselves:
they offer no proof.

Proof is no longer possible when the bird's
flight is random or guided by gravity,
when we think in neural networks. They stir
us as wind chimes are moved to sing sweetly,

mechanically by forces that appear concerned.
How is it possible to let them guide our love
when they themselves are wired to each other,
a tangle of marionettes in a dark theater?

As It Was in the Beginning

I raise an alternative from the jug
and bakery shop—yeast, bubbling,
ignoring their conjugal selves

for solitary acts involving
templates, nucleic acids,
replicons and the sizzle of birth—

God releasing Adam asexually
across the dome of the world,
His index finger flicking Adam off

as we might reject a former lover.
The world budding from spherical deities
filled with DNA and histones—

protrusions on smooth surfaces—
at first less than hemispheres
bulging in apparent stasis, while inside

a potpourri of chemicals churns out
what many believe are perfect copies
of the Lord; later, each, set free,

a homunculus rotating in the void,
creating a gravity of its own,
singing hosannahs in a beery breath.

They deserve all manner praise—

cymbals, hymns, prayers and masses,
temples, shrines, cathedrals.

For what is more precise and marvelous
than unequal scission that recites
the whole of creation, perhaps forever?

Michael Lieberman

Michael Lieberman was born and raised in Pittsburgh, PA. A graduate of Yale College, he holds medical and doctoral degrees from the University of Pittsburgh. He is a research pathologist interested in the molecular basis of disease, and he chairs the Department of Pathology at Baylor College of Medicine in Houston. More than thirty years elapsed between the publication of his first poems in a high school literary magazine and the appearance of his mature work in national magazines and journals. In 1991 he was co-winner of the Houston Poetry Fest's Juried Competition, and Thorn Books brought out his chapbook *Praising with my Body* in 1992. *A History of the Sweetness of the World* is his first full-length collection. He is married to Susan Abel Lieberman, a nonfiction writer; they have two grown sons.

Jacket design and art by Mark Piñón
Photograph by Carol Rowe DeBender